Food Chains and Webs

Ocean
Food Chains

Angela Royston

Heinemann
LIBRARY

Chicago, Illinois

Edited by Claire Throp, Diyan Leake and Helen
Cox Cannons
Designed by Joanna Malivoire and Philippa
Jenkins
Original illustrations © Capstone Global
Library Ltd 2014
Picture research by Elizabeth Alexander and
Tracy Cummins
Production by Victoria Fitzgerald
Originated by Capstone Global Library Ltd

**Library of Congress Cataloging-in-
Publication Data**
Royston, Angela, 1945- author.
  Ocean food chains / Angela Royston.
    pages cm.—(Food chains and webs)
  Includes bibliographical references and index.
  ISBN 978-1-4846-0517-2 (hb)—ISBN 978-1-
4846-0524-0 (pb) 1. Marine ecology—Juvenile
literature. 2. Food chains (Ecology)—Juvenile
literature. 3. Marine animals—Juvenile literature.
4. Wildlife conservation—Juvenile literature. I.
Title.
  QH541.5.S3
  577.7—dc23   2013040534

Acknowledgments
We would like to thank the following for
permission to reproduce photographs:
Alamy pp. 9, 17d (© National Geographic
Image Collection), 10 (© Ron Chapple Stock),
11e, 17e (© Kelvin Aitken/VWPICS), 15 (©
Dinodia Photos), 22 (© WaterFrame), 23b,
25 snapper (© David Fleetham); Corbis pp.
11b (© Norbert Wu/Minden Pictures), 12 (©
Visuals Unlimited), 19 (© Ralph Lee Hopkins);
FLPA p. 17c (Norbert Wu/Minden Pictures);
Getty Images pp. 14 (Paul Souders), 23d, 25
coral (Oxford Scientific); Shutterstock pp. 1 (©
Vlad61), 4 (© tororo reaction), 5 (© cdelacy), 7,
13, 29 (© Ethan Daniels), 8 (© BigRoloImages),
11a (© aldorado), 11c (© Leonardo Gonzalez),
11d (© Lebendkulturen.de), 16 (© Incredible
Arctic), 17a (© qingqing), 17b (© AleksandrN),
18 (© Dray van Beeck), 20 (© BioLife Pics),
21 (© Solodov Alexey), 23a, 23c, 25 butterfly
fish, 25 shark (© Greg Amptman), 24, 25 turtle
(© Isabelle Kuehn), 25 parrotfish (© stephan
kerkhofs), 25 seagrass (© Rich Carey), 25
seaweed (© iofoto), 27 (© Mark Medcalf), 28 (©
kolyvanov); Superstock p. 26 (age fotostock).

Cover photograph of a green turtle eating a red
jellyfish reproduced with permission of Getty
Images (© Ai Angel Gentel).

We would like to thank Michael Bright for his
invaluable help in the preparation of this book.

Every effort has been made to contact copyright
holders of material reproduced in this book.
Any omissions will be rectified in subsequent
printings if notice is given to the publisher.

Contents

Some words are shown in bold, **like this.**
You can find out what they mean by
looking in the glossary.

Living in the Oceans

Oceans may look bare, but under the surface is an amazing living world. Most sea animals live in shallow water around the coasts, but some live in deep water farther out to sea.

Oceans are huge and deep, except close to the coasts.

A great white shark feeds on seals, fish, and even other sharks.

Sea animals include tiny shrimps, fish, and huge whales. This book looks at what they eat and how they survive.

Where Are the Oceans?

The map below gives the names of the different oceans in the world. The coldest waters are in the Arctic and Southern Oceans. The warmest waters are on each side of the Equator.

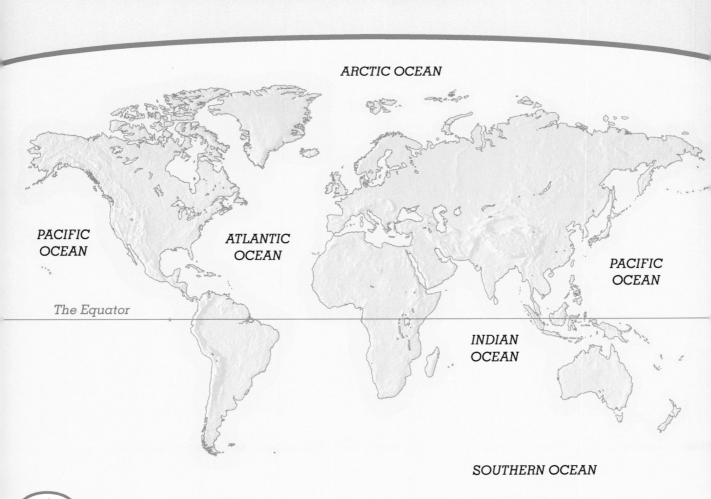

ARCTIC OCEAN

PACIFIC OCEAN

ATLANTIC OCEAN

PACIFIC OCEAN

The Equator

INDIAN OCEAN

SOUTHERN OCEAN

World's largest ocean

The Pacific Ocean covers a larger area than all the **continents** put together.

Coral reefs are home to millions of sea animals.

What Is a Food Chain?

All living things need food to survive. Food gives them **energy** to live, grow, and move.

Penguins use their wings to swim and to keep their balance.

Krill swim together in large groups.

A **food chain** shows how the energy in food passes from one living thing to another. For example, when a penguin eats **krill**, the penguin's body breaks down the krill to get energy.

An Atlantic Food Chain

The **food chain** on page 11 is from the Atlantic coast of North America. It shows how **energy** passes from microscopic **plankton** through tiny animals called **copepods** to herring. It then passes to squid and, finally, to a dolphin.

This is the Atlantic Ocean off Florida.

Food chain

A dolphin feeds on a squid

A squid catches a herring

A herring feeds on a copepod

A copepod feeds on plankton

Plankton is made up of tiny living things

Where Do Food Chains Begin?

Ocean **food chains** begin with **plankton**. Plankton is made up of tiny animals and plant-like living things that float near the surface of the water.

This is what plankton looks like under a microscope.

Seaweed is a type of **alga**, which also makes its own food.

The tiny, plant-like living things are called phytoplankton, and they use the **energy** of sunlight to make their own food. The tiny animals are called zooplankton, and they feed on the plants.

Sea Animals

Many kinds of sea animals feed on **plankton**. They include jellyfish and **krill**. The blue whale is the largest animal that has ever lived, and it feeds on huge amounts of krill and **copepods**.

A jellyfish floats through the water.

Big fish, such as these tuna, feed on smaller fish.

Animals that feed on other animals are called **carnivores**. Large carnivores, such as tuna fish, hunt many types of smaller fish, including shoals of young bluefish.

An Arctic Food Chain

Some sea animals live in the icy waters near the Arctic and Antarctic. This is an Arctic **food chain**. It shows how **energy** passes from the **plankton** through the **krill** to the cod. It then passes to the seal and on to the killer whale.

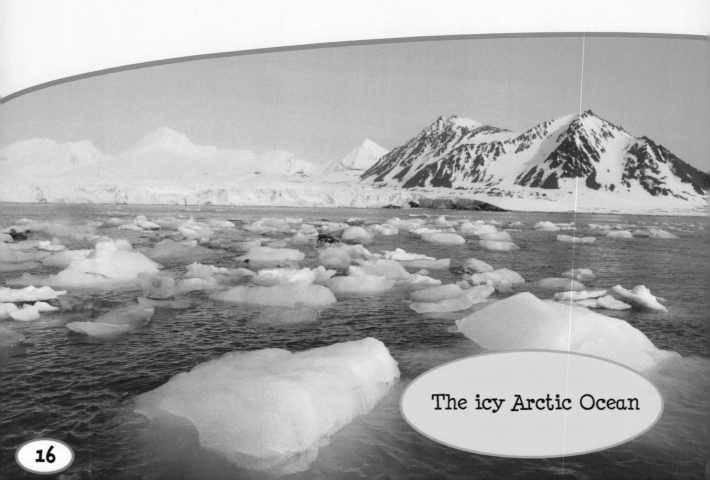

The icy Arctic Ocean

Food chain

A killer whale catches a seal

A seal feeds on a cod

A cod swallows tiny krill

Krill feed on plankton

Phytoplankton provide food for krill

Top Predators

A killer whale is at the top of the Arctic **food chain.** No ocean animal dares to attack it. Some sharks, such as mako sharks, are among the top **predators** in other oceans.

A blue shark is a top predator in cool and tropical seas.

A polar bear is a top predator in its food chain.

There are fewer top predators than other sea animals. Each link in a food chain needs lots of **prey** in the link below it to survive.

Living Off the Remains

Some **predators** are also **scavengers**, which means that they feed off the remains of dead animals.

This coral crab lives in the Caribbean Sea.

Amphipods are scavengers. They look for remains at the bottom of oceans.

Crabs, lobsters, and many other animals that live at the bottom of the oceans are scavengers. They eat the remains of dead animals that sink to the seabed. These animals help to recycle waste.

Coral Reef Food Chain

About a quarter of all known types of sea animals live around coral reefs. The coral reef itself is made by tiny animals called **coral polyps**. The **food chain** on page 23 is for a coral reef in Hawaii.

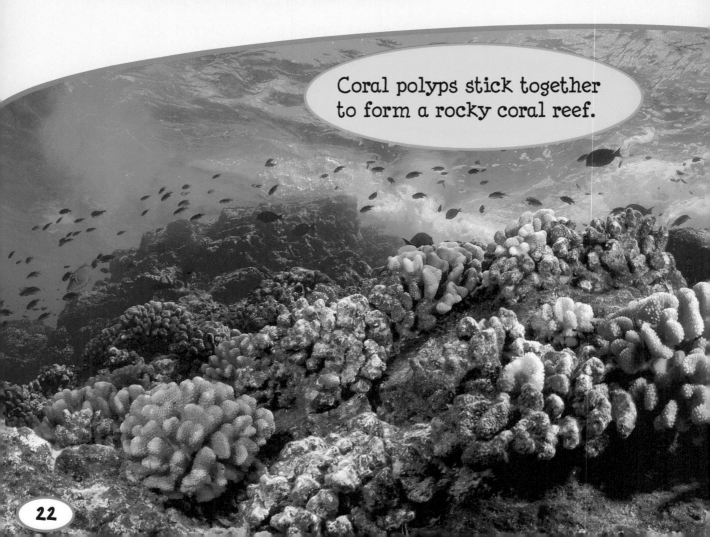

Coral polyps stick together to form a rocky coral reef.

Food chain

A tiger shark is a top **predator**. It preys on a snapper.

A snapper catches a young butterfly fish

A butterfly fish feeds on the coral polyps

Plankton that live inside coral polyps provide the polyps with food

Food Webs

A **food web** shows how different **food chains** link together. On page 25, this food web shows how some sea animals on the coral reef compete for the same food and may be in danger from several **predators**.

Green turtles are often found near coral reefs where seagrass also grows.

Food web

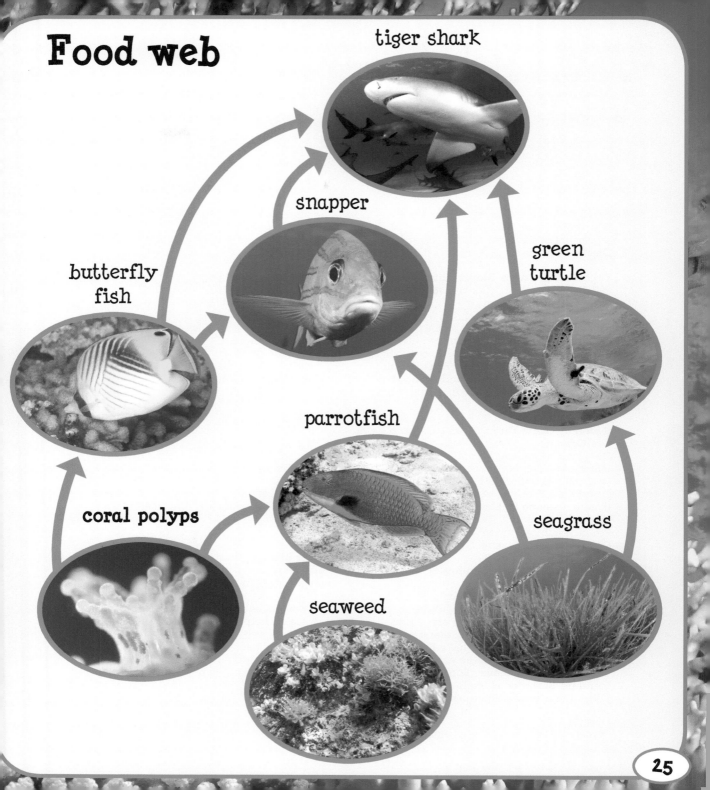

tiger shark

snapper

butterfly fish

green turtle

parrotfish

coral polyps

seagrass

seaweed

Broken Chains

When one part of a **food chain** is damaged, the whole chain can break down. Many fish and seabirds feed on sand eels. However, sand eels are becoming scarce in the North Atlantic, mainly because people are catching too many of them.

Sand eels are food for many ocean animals.

Puffins feed their young on sand eels.

It is now harder for animals higher up the North Atlantic food chain, such as puffins, to survive.

Protecting Food Chains

Many **food chains** are in danger of breaking down. One reason is that huge fishing trawlers are catching too many fish and destroying ocean **habitats**.

Fishing trawlers take huge amounts of fish from the sea.

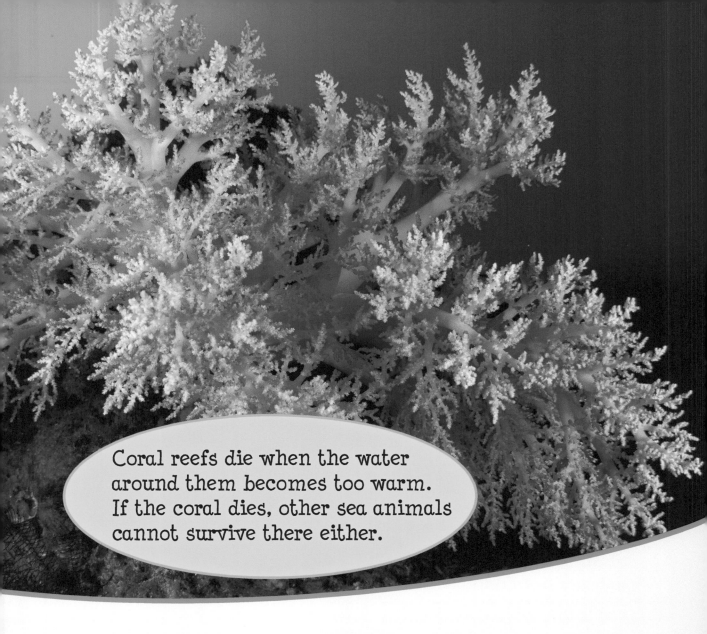

Coral reefs die when the water around them becomes too warm. If the coral dies, other sea animals cannot survive there either.

One solution is to make marine reserves. These are areas of ocean where fishing is banned.

Glossary

alga tiny living thing, for example, green slime. Algae can make their own food.

carnivore animal that eats only the meat of other animals

continent large area of land

copepod tiny creature similar to a water flea

coral polyp small sea animal that sticks together in clumps. Some types of polyp build stony "houses," one on top of the other, to form a hard coral reef.

energy power needed to do something, such as move, breathe, or swallow

food chain diagram that shows how energy passes from plants to different animals

food web diagram that shows how different plants and animals in a habitat are linked by what they eat

habitat place where something lives

krill tiny shrimp that feeds on plankton

plankton tiny animals and plant-like living things that float near the surface of water

predator animal that hunts other animals for food

prey animal hunted for food

scavenger animal that feeds off the flesh and remains of dead animals

Find Out More

Books

Facthound offers a safe, fun way to find web sites related to this book. All the sites on Facthound have been researched by our staff.

Here's all you do:

Visit www.facthound.com

Type in this code: 9781484605172

Web sites

www.greatbarrierreef.com.au/information/great-barrier-reef-food-web
Find out about food chains and a food web on Australia's Great Barrier Reef from this informative web site.

kids.nationalgeographic.co.uk/kids/activities/new/ocean
This web site includes videos, games, and photos as well as information about the oceans.

wwf.panda.org/about_our_earth/ecoregions/about/habitat_types/habitats/oceans/
Learn more about ocean life at this WWF site.

Index